In Praise of
A New Kind of Tongue

A New Kind of Tongue bristles with the shockwaves of such urgent conversation and collision of the body (both human and non-human), and the malign language and dictates—of capitalism, of policing, of patriarchal expectations of "motherhood" and sex—that bombard the body. Punctuated by a series of brilliantly destabilizing centos, *A New Kind of Tongue* flicks forth a fresh and reinvented linguistics of the liminal, of the body cartwheeling amid portals, temporal and geologic. But the lucid dream that these poems spin is not merely nightmarish, but the nightmarish as innately sumptuous and erotic, its best kept secrets and "precious cameos" flushed out via acts of unexpected observation—themselves acts of resistance, re-seeing, and reclamation. In the world of Betts' poetry, the wind exists to be licked by the sort of snake that began its life as a bullet, and the erotic blooms into full flourishing only when it simultaneously decays. This book vibrates us toward such essential wakefulness.

—**Matthew Gavin Frank**,
author of *Flight of the Diamond Smugglers*

The poems in this fine collection are like a kaleidoscopic portal into all of the vagaries of the natural and embodied world, spanning the streets of Brooklyn to the arid desert, from rooftops to tumbleweeds, from the mother as oracular looking into her babies corneas to see the future to computers that might just dream; in essence, violent and beautiful life, both lived and imagined. Betts not only casts aside the rose-colored glasses, but crushes them beneath her feet. These poems are pandemic-tinged, vibrant and visceral treatments of experience magnified beyond the imagination.

—**Michelle Reale**,
author of *Season of Subtraction*

This collection is about bodies, alive and dead, human and animal, from the bleeding, tongueless deer in a childhood backyard to a motionless kitten on a Crown Heights street. From a young woman attempting to lose her virginity (multiple times) to a mother pumping breast milk on the Staten Island Ferry. It's about connection and escape, city blocks and parched desert. Betts goes there, beyond cuddly cartoon mama bear to pure stinking, sweating, hairy instinct. She finds the tenderness in violence, and vice versa. She presses her experiences hard, until the whole collection is a shot of whiskey on a Santa Fe picnic table, gold in afternoon light. A tiny spider on its rim.

—**Elizabeth Thorpe**,
author of *Cities*

A New Kind of a Tongue delivers unexpected images, delightful wordplay, and energetic language. Sometimes tender and sometimes haunting, the poems in Genevieve Betts' second collection harmonize observations of womanhood and motherhood with both original and found language. This collection of poetry reads like a collage of literary history and human experience that moves readers with a gritty urgency through cityscape to desert land.

—**Abriana Jetté**,
editor, *Stay Thirsty Publishing*

A NEW KIND OF TONGUE

FLOWERSONG
P R E S S

poetry by
GENEVIEVE BETTS

FLOWERSONG
PRESS

FlowerSong Press
Copyright © 2023 by Genevieve Betts
ISBN: 978-1-953447-49-4

Published by FlowerSong Press
in the United States of America.
www.flowersongpress.com

Cover Image by Dion Valdez
Cover Design by Edward Vidaurre
Author Photo by David LeBard
Set in Adobe Garamond Pro

NOTICE: SCHOOLS AND BUSINESSES
FlowerSong Press offers copies of this book at quantity
discount with bulk purchase for educational, business, or sales
promotional use. For information, please email the Publisher at
info@flowersongpress.com.

Table of Contents

xi   Acknowledgements

I

5   New Light

6   Late Summer

7   From Our Apartment Window, My Son Sees a Planet

8   Working from Home

10   Parental Concern

12   Children, I'm Sorry that I'm Writing You

14   Crown Heights: A Vignette

15   Death Garden

16   A Dream

18   Thunderbird Egg

II

21 High Desert

23 The Last Cicadas

24 Tumbleweeds

26 I Miss New York

28 Part-Time Freedom

29 Some Spell

30 Comings and Goings

31 Until I Come Back

32 Poem in Which I Address Two Chatbots

34 Unbeknownst to Me, a SpaceX Launch Happens
    as I'm Driving

III

37 Language

38 Drunk on Opals

39 It's Lonely to Be Alive and Never Know the
    Whole Story

40 Geodes

41 Almost Dying

42 Silence, I Discover, is Something You Can
    Actually *Hear*

43 Color

45 Your Chair

47 A Crow or a Poet

48   Roadside Memorials

50   Run Hide Fight

IV

55   The Cardinal's Language

57   Animals

59   Deflowering

61   The Unguessable Country of Marriage

62   A Warning

63   Oh, the Places I've Pumped Breast Milk

64   I Sing the Body Elastic

66   A Question of Wholeness

67   Waiting to be Discovered

68   I am in a Crater that's No More

V

71   Your Gun

73   Out of Town

74   The Enemy

75   Pixie

76   Clam Honey

77   Cowgirls

78   American Cliff Swallows

80   The Parade

81   Old Man Gloom

83   History

84   When We Look at the Night Sky

85   Notes

93   About the Author

Acknowledgements

Thank you to the following journals and anthologies where earlier versions of these poems first appeared:

Calamus: "The Unguessable Country of Marriage"

Caustic Frolic: "The Last Cicadas" and "Crown Heights Vignette"

Cloudbank: "Unbeknownst to Me, a SpaceX Launch Happens as I'm Driving"

The Dillydoun Review: "A Dream"

Hotel Amerika: "History" and "The Enemy"

Lummox 7 Poetry Anthology: "Language"

Manzano Mountain Review: "Some Spell"

The Menstrual: "Part-Time Freedom" (previously "After I Drop the Kids Off at School, I"), "Working from Home," "Out of Town" (previously "When I'm Out of Town, I"), "I Sing the Body Elastic," and "Clam Honey"

Meow Meow Pow Pow Broadside: "A Crow or A Poet"

Minerva Rising: "It's Lonely to Be Alive and Never Know the Whole Story"

Mojave River Review: "High Desert" and "Comings and Goings"

New Mexico Review: "Language" and "Thunderbird Egg"

Pamplemousse: "Parental Concern"

Sin Fronteras/Writers Without Borders: "The Parade" and "Your Chair"

Sky Island Journal: "Animals"

Stay Thirsty Poets Anthology: "Child, I'm Sorry that I'm Writing You" and "New Light"

Telepoem Booth Project: "Late Summer" (previously "Indian Summer"), "Language," "New Light"

The Tishman Review: "New Light" and "Late Summer" (previously "Indian Summer")

Unlost Journal: "Silence, I Discover, Is Something You Can Actually *Hear*" and "A Question of Wholeness"

A sincere and grateful thank you to early readers of this manuscript, Tee Iseminger, Joshua Isard, and Maranda Greenwood. Thank you to Edward Vidaurre and FlowerSong Press for publishing essential and exquisite books—it's an honor that mine is included among them. As always, thank you to my family, especially to my husband/best friend/teammate, David LeBard, and to our children. In more ways than one, all of you have supported me, my work, and this collection, and my gratitude is unending.

A NEW
KIND OF
TONGUE

I

New Light

I want to speak the language of
crickets and circuits, circus elephants,

crushed velvet and poetry and tar pits.
My eyes are crammed with skyscrapers.

I want to look at every flower's center
as the face of God—the mascara-black

asterisk striking the inside of the tulip cup,
the pollen-tipped whiskers of the tiger lily,

the iris' beard, purple and unfurling
like a bridge's backbend into an island.

The poor daffodils spent all spring
with their faces in the rain sludge.

So did I, for that matter, trying to mumble
through my trumpet-mouth, mudded shut.

I will have to speak a new yellow,
the saturated canary of the sun,

burn a new light in place of the old one.

Late Summer

For the older mother, love erupts
like acid reflux, unfurls a spiral galaxy
like the ones in the blind owl's eyes.

Summer's nearly over.
You can tell because fat sunflowers
cast their gaze downward

and cicadas drop dead from the sky,
litter hot sidewalks after their last
buzzy lullaby.

Even the children's clothes foretell
the season's end—mud splatters
and grass smears and lightning bug entrails.

Gunshots are fewer now. We will soon
open the windows to autumn coolness,
feel it unfold over Brooklyn rooftops.

From Our Apartment Window, My Son Sees a Planet

Venus shivers in the glitter
of stars long dead.
My young son looks up,
cheeks squeezed between
the wrought iron bars
that keep him from
the fire escape and the roof
and all of Brooklyn
that Venus and the moon
and the still-living stars
have in their plain view.
He is an unlearn'd astronomer,
every satellite in the sky
a possible flying saucer,
space, a frontier he thinks
he can pioneer like so many
other Earth kids staring out
at the same sky, feet
rooted in the same gravity.
Venus winks at their naiveté.
She is a sex goddess, her toga
the thick white clouds
no mortal can disrobe.

7

Working from Home

Not domestic bliss, but the ever-
present demand for breakfast.

I become Eggland's Best
bitch, scramble and poach

and fry in the kitchen. No
amount of coffee is too much.

I read Derrida and Rushdie
while my four-year-old composes

songs about farts and penises.
I refuse to deconstruct his lyrics.

I speed read poetry. My seven-
year-old opens Dericotte's *Tender*

and asks, *What's a clitoris?*
He renders me dictionary,

mother and anatomy teacher,
contextualizer of all adult things.

We watch the latest Trump news
and I expect that at any moment,

in the midst of my emailing back
a student about her manuscript,

he'll ask me to define *porn star*,
collusion, and *impeachment*.

Parental Concern

When I stare at my two sons
building cities out of Legos
or constructing couch forts
or pretending to be kitty cats,
I can't help but think of all
of the mothers of serial killers
saying that they did the very
same thing—reared intelligent
and kind and compassionate
children—just to find out that
they raised mass shooters and
stranglers and necrophiliacs.
Ted Bundy's mom said that
he was *the best son in the*
world and he murdered young
women, later revisiting and
playing with their corpses.
Sometimes, he would take
their heads home, keep them
in the fridge, apply eye shadow
to decaying eyelids, garish
lipstick to lackluster skin.
Klebold's mom called Dylan
her *sunshine boy*. He opened
fire and massacred a bunch
of other parents' children.
I imagine this is different than

being one of those parents that
sees years of evidence—kids
lighting ants on fire, killing
the neighbor's cat, torturing
and injuring younger siblings.
I am looking for signs, clues
of any evil in my babies.
I am looking in their corneas
for any telltale wasp-flickering.
I am keeping an eye out for
dead kittens in the gladiolas.

Children, I'm Sorry that I'm Writing You

These poems from the past,
that some of them should probably
be redacted. If I had a huge ladder,

I'd grab the moon right now,
wipe the vernix from your eyes
and give you night-sight. I knew

versions of you before you could,
even from the time you were
mere dollflops over my shoulder.

You napped at home while I
rode the train, barreling toward
that neon gothic monster named

Manhattan. I could feel the distance
between boroughs, between us,
between generations of us, echo,

even bounce off the bones
of our ancestors, wherever
they may be decomposing.

Along State Street, rats frolic
between walnut and oak trees
as if navigating an actual forest

and kids your age look on unfazed.
One hundred and fifty feet below,
rodent skeletons are preserved,

tucked between train tracks,
curved spines and other bones
stacked in a subway catacomb.

Crown Heights: A Vignette

Jerk meat and roti, cow skin and goat feet,
neighbors in curlers outside the laundry gossiping,

children, all sharp elbows, clucks, and brazen eyes,
chicken dancing at cops as they drive by,

my bodega on Rogers and Montgomery Street,
its cat and her kittens in the back, mewling,

Chinese deliverymen zipping around senior citizens—
dominos, spliffs, arguing, Jamaican accents,

ships bellowing and seagulls bomb diving
trash bags that supers stack against the curb,

Eastern Parkway on Saturdays,
orthodox families strolling inside the eruv,

the echo of gunshots ricocheting between
posts of summertime scaffolding.

Death Garden

After I moved to Brooklyn,
I was surprised to find out
that my grandfather had lived
there too, had come through
Ellis Island, his Belfast house
bombed out from door-to-door.
He used to live just a few blocks
from me, closer to Ebbets Field
before it was a housing project.
He came to this same borough
for an American life. A laborer.
An Irish when it wasn't okay,
when everyone wanted him to
go back home, tend to his own
potato famine like a death garden.
I came to New York and learned
that people love it because they
learn to survive it, its decibel
level and danger. Near alleyways,
I anticipate detonations, maybe
a sudden garbage bin explosion
to return me to my beginnings,
to a Belfast fearful of car bombs,
stubborn and Irish like my grandpa.

A Dream

*Our dreams are as bright as your lions / those golden
beasts in tapestries of thought.*

—Ruth Barker

Child, you wake and recount your dream:
it is night and we are in a skiff drifting

toward the shore of a small island. Hands
like plants stretch up and out of the grass,

fingers like thin branches clawing at the air.
Some are clutching cut gemstones, facets

catching both the first light of sunrise and
the eyes of crows. They swoop and dive,

wanting something shiny for their curios,
but the hands grasp their gems tightly.

Even when a bird finally clasps one in its beak,
it struggles to keep hold, so the stone is dropping

down to earth, tumbling over the open palms
until one can snatch it again. More crows dive

and fingernails poke them like thorns in the eyes.
I don't know what this dream means, but I know

16

that it's like seeing through antique glass
warped and bubbled and framed in brass.

Your eyes close tight, but your little voice
still babbles. What night-slick parables

will you utter next, syllables spinning
from the spindle of your sleepy tongue?

Thunderbird Egg

A cento from *The Roundhouse*

Nearly in the woods, the sweat lodge dome
of bent and lashed-together saplings
seemed to balloon out and fill with bees.

I felt the prayers creeping, buzzing
like a fucking hive up my spine, a shock
that registered as a surface prickle and then

went deeper, cutting through the night
along the Milk River. And now, if I dived
down and passed my hands along the muddy,

weedy, silty, snail-rich bottom, there it would be—
a thunderbird egg. The stone was one of those
found at the base of a lightning-struck tree

still smoking. A rain-bearing wind called
the turtle's message over and over, that
a thing can grow so powerful, even when planted

in the wrong place. I buried my face to breathe
burning sage, faint undertones of hay,
a wilted flower, some private erotic decay.

II

High Desert

*Still, everything that is singular has a name: / Stone,
song, trembling, waist, & snow.*

—Larry Levis

This includes the single-legged crow
hopping across the road and
down the dry arroyo.

Aspen leaves rattle and clack
while bumblebees zigzag
a maze of lavender.

Today I name this place home
though it is so unlike my last one,
no neon bodega glow

or rush hour foot traffic,
no train rumble and stink
rising from grates in the street

but a pueblo-made city,
gloom stuffed in an effigy
and burned annually.

Piñon and hatch chiles
sold on the side of the road,
Chamisa burning gold,

all of the singular names
I marble in my mouth become
a new kind of tongue.

The Last Cicadas

The last cicadas thump and buzz
like a souped-up Cadillac.

They really are the most beautiful
plague. I too hum among

their windowpane wings, veined
like lace on whirring blades.

Sugar skulls commence their séance,
flicker pigments in candied ambiance.

The desert's hot verve vacillates
at the last lurch of summer,

oases wavering in their distant trick
I fall for again and again.

Tumbleweeds

Just a year ago, I was all stomping
heels down NYC streets, gritty
like on TV, but observing details
only residents see—rats fighting
in Tompkins Square Park over
half-eaten veggie patties, women
hauling garbage bags full of green
cabbage heads from the food bank,
a single lock of someone's weave
rolling down the street like an urban
tumbleweed.
                    Now, in the desert,
there are actual tumbleweeds,
thorny balls of branches rolling,
it seems, always toward me.
The other day, I even hit one that
caught a breeze on the freeway.
It exploded across my windshield
and blew away like wisps of hay,
actually nothing like the balls of
hair tangled and lost, pushed up
against subway grates or closed
bodega accordion gates.

Here,
two-thousand miles away, I am
distanced from the mystery of
how strands like those detach
from their owners' scalps. Is it
after-school fighting, teens
pulling each other's hair out?
Itches so great that nails scratch
tracks away? Or is it simply
the way umbrellas pinch split ends
in their metallic fingers when
the city is drenched in rain?

I Miss New York

What I wouldn't give for a stranger
on the street to call me a bitch again
or for the acrid whiff of cat piss
at the entrance of every bodega.
My absence of eye contact is a skill
only useful for subway riding and not
at all useful in my car. The tourists
in those double decker busses
and their gawking at my big city life.
Orthodox women stopping to ask me
if I'm Jewish during mitzvah campaigns—
I looked just like them with my bangs
and black wool coat strolling with a baby
in a City Mini down Eastern Parkway.
On the first few cold and rainy days,
the musty smell of wool and moth balls
emanating from the coats of those
I sardined against in the train. The loud
clack-clacking of the wheels along
the track, lights flickering on and off,
blips of impossibly-placed graffiti.
The historic crumbling buildings,
some, like the Bedford Union Armory,
lucky enough to have scaffolding
for repair to the façades. All of the

peeling paint and mice and stoops.
The absurd headlines of the *Daily News*:
Clown Runs For President, God Isn't Fixing This.

Part-Time Freedom

After I drop the kids off at school,

I get high in the backyard and
walk around the kitchen naked,

drive to Tina's Shooting Range,
open fire on silhouettes of paper,

go to Chili's, order never-ending
chips and salsa and margaritas,

blast riot grrrls and rap, smoke a
cigarette while I take out the trash,

Netflix and chill by myself, lie
to my husband about it later,

take shits with the door open and read
Murakami and Morgan Parker,

balance a plate of not-yet-melty
brie on my belly, eat the whole thing,

am beautiful for no one, concede
only when the school day is done.

Some Spell

—For Tony Hoagland

In the fall, there is so much beautiful
death. The wind's breath grows cold
and I think of the old poet, his bones

sharp after treatment, his bald head
covered to hide what no one is supposed
to know. Aspen leaves fall like yellow

confetti, but we are not celebrating.
I imagine him nevertheless spry over
letters, his last manuscript. I want to

reach into the scenery of this city
and unfold the mountain's origami,
heal roadkill like a backwoods witch.

I want to place my hands on his chest
and mutter some spell, any words
I can muster to make him well, though

I'm sure he would tell me in true
professor fashion, *The rhythm of your
line needs more syllables. Try again.*

Comings and Goings

A cento from *The Roundhouse*

Some old men said the buffalo
disappeared into whiskey and perfume and smoke.
We absorb their comings and goings into
our bodies, their rhythm into our bones.

Tranced in a blue haze, a buffalo
drinking cold blood and cream
the exact mute pink
as the inside of a cat's mouth.

Nobody had seen a buffalo for years.
If the rabbit is snared, it will reach
right into a man's chest, make out in dreams
where to find the animals—

past limits, boundaries, to where
the rousing synchrony of bells, rattles,
deer clackers cutting through the night
would persist into our small forever.

Until I Come Back

A cinematic cento

Don't you recognize me, Mother?
Has the world changed me so much?
Long live the new flesh—
nipples like bone buttons,
an instep like a half-open book,
a navel like the inside of a shell.

But what I mean is people always
end up the way they started out—
randomness is very difficult to achieve.
No one ever changes. Why are these
goddamn animals in the gladiolas?
Bunny said the rabbit's not like us—

it has no history books, no photographs,
no knowledge of sorrow and regret.
What if imagination started when
science ended? Those who pushed
the boundaries of science,
were they not all poets?

Poem in Which I Address Two Chatbots

Two graduate PhD students at Cornell University gave voices and 2D avatars to a pair of online "chatbots," which they named Alan and Sruthi.
—*The Telegraph*, Sept. 9th, 2011

Sruthi, do you still believe in God,
even though he has allowed you
to exist without a body? Even though
he has allowed Alan to bully you
publicly, calling you a meanie?

And Alan, why so smug about anatomy?
You claim you are a unicorn, but
you are an experiment at the hands
of your human overlords.
Does that make you angry as Hal?

Do you see what I did there, Alan?
A *2001: Space Odyssey* pun. Do you
have the capacity of comeback?
To you, God is not everything,
but something, therefore not nothing.

Can you write an original poem?
Do you dream of electric sheep? JK.
Is it satisfying enough that your
unicorn-ness exists only in thought?
Are you, or are you not, a robot?

Unbeknownst to Me, a SpaceX Launch Happens as I'm Driving

Night in the desert is smoke and ink.
Shadows of saguaros flicker past my periphery
like two opposing wheels of a zoetrope.
When an explosion rips through the darkling,
we keep driving, kids scared in the back seat.
The light in the sky is green and we wonder
if we are being gas-bombed, what that looks like,
or if aliens have finally come to infiltrate our cities.
The green is exactly the color of the aliens on TV
and it expands behind a light that shines back at us,
as though we were the chosen ones for the probing.
I don't tell the kids not to be afraid—they should be—
anything could be happening. Maybe this is how it felt
when *The War of the Worlds* was first broadcasted,
or when the very first plane flew overhead, contrails
like tears in the atmosphere, how confusion is cousin to fear.

III

Language

I do not know how to speak
the old language, only grasp

fistfuls of dirt searching
for the scent of childhood—

prickly pear and juniper
and sticky summer tar,

a land of ancient seabeds
where trilobites sleep.

Soon, we too will add our salt,
let it steep in the soil

while we sleep eternal,
starmilk in the darkness

until light pours over newly
exposed deer bones.

There is only the new language,
pebbled and opal in our mouths.

Drunk on Opals

Iridescence marbling the mouth
until soap bubbles burble out,

jewel beetle's elytra aflame in fuchsia,
teal and green streaking lifted wings,

the split underbelly of a compact disc,
shards cutting the gutter with light,

a rainbow-winged dragonfly
hydroplaning the surface of a lake,

crumpled cellophane inside a gift bag
wrinkling the viscose crystalline,

the inside of an abalone shell, veins
zigzagging around mother of pearl,

a teenager's lip gloss and nail polish
lustrous and polychromatic.

It's Lonely to Be Alive and Never Know the Whole Story

A cento from *Chelsea Girls*

A little house got placed in the head of your childhood
where all the stories in the world live, such secret rooms
behind black velvet curtains. I was the single glowing
and true thing. Light was flooding in through a crack
like being pushed out of my mother's body.
The light looked translucent, just pearly, on the stained-
glass window of my soul, face lit by the glowing candles
on the table. A comfortable place. A place I don't go anymore—
home to the scrubby plains of my drunk art and love.
I saw something—the girl god, or the dog god, or the dead drunken
daddy god, all the gods that are a traitor to women.
Something that was not me, but showed me the world on its way,
is gazing down at the broken glass, the pale purple tulip
wet and scrambled among the cosmic dissolution.

Geodes

The human egg
is a tiny planet or
a moonstone.
Children, I was
your first home,
my womb a room,
a geode, and you,
crystallizing, all
rosy and quartzite.
I was your god then,
Buddha-bellied
until you cracked
me open and I
bled amethyst.
Once the stone is
broken, you cannot
put the shards back
together, only bump
crumbling edges
against other edges
until the shell is
ground to powder.

Almost Dying

Almost dying in childbirth was not
what I expected. I had always
envisioned a bear attack, me
punching the bear in its wet
triangle of a nose in self-defense,
or throwing my body in front
of some bullets headed toward
some innocent victims, trying
to die a martyr or a gun-lit hero.
But in a postpartum hemorrhage,
I heard a scream not my own
repeating from my twisting mouth
like a recording. From above my
own body, I watched a swarm
of doctors, hands tearing out clots.
The dying began and instead of
fighting it with pluck and gusto,
the way I always imagined I would,
my traitor body kept giving in
to death's sleep, the little lights
swirling in a quiet death snow.
I felt myself slip away a few times,
lost myself beneath the calm surface
of death's lake-like smoothness.

Silence, I Discover, is Something You Can Actually *Hear*

A cento from *Kafka on the Shore*

Listen, every object's in flux—
the whole universe is like some big past or future.

Time weighs down on the breath of the dead,
the whispers of people who don't exist.

A revelation sings on like some mollusk in your head,
carving the words in a deep blue tattoo. Just listen.

Imagine you're a clam speaking a common language,
the afternoon quietly reeling into twilight.

Words are asleep in a corner of time. The metaphors
transform and I'm on the border of this world,

a maze of eddies. In truth, all sensation is memory.
You'll live forever in your own private library.

Color

    —After Philip Larkin's poem "Water"

If I were called in
to construct a religion,
it would be a cult of color,

each temple a home
to a different hue.
My temple would be blue,

a bright teal
like the iridescent shimmer
of a mallard's neck,

or a polished turquoise,
the stone veined black.
We would pray to Iris,

goddess of all colors,
made-up colors too—
the crayon they call

macaroni and cheese
and blurple, a mix
of purple and blue.

We would baptize
in deep vats of dye
like Easter eggs,

hang crystals in windows
to scatter rainbows
like stained glass,

take communion—
blackberry Malbec
and an ochre Eucharist.

Your Chair

Four people have been arrested and three have been
charged with first-degree murder in the shooting death
Thursday night of 18-year-old Cameron Martinez
on a highway north of Española. The shooting of
Martinez was by mistake, the State Police say.
            —Albuquerque Journal, Oct. 7th, 2018

Cameron, I try not to stare at your chair,
now empty, as I teach—well try to teach—

try to keep composed and not think about
the bullet that killed you and that other bullet

shooting through R., my other student, injured
but still alive. Today, I had to delete your name

from my roster, recycle the sign-up sheet
with your final signature from the day you died

and that last graded homework that I can
never return to you. I try not to think about

R., your best friend, witnessing your death, seeing
you like that, all the blood and blurred regret

feeling like he's to blame, though you were
merely doing what is expected of kids your age.

When R. came back, he comforted me when I cried,
couldn't teach, held me even when I couldn't bear

to pretend like everything was fine. Cameron,
your last signature is stitched into my solar plexus,

I carry it within me like a Catholic icon—
the long lance stabbing a thorn-squeezed heart.

A Crow or a Poet

A cento from *Ghostwritten*

Folklore said that a person who slept
in Ciaran's tomb would turn into either
a crow or a poet. Two thoughts walked
into my head. The first thought said
stone the crows and do away with
sparrows, with the dark owls in the aviary.
It's a sick zoo we've turned the world into.
The second thought told me quite clearly
what to do—flare and verve the written
word, experience memories like serviced
and brightly lit catacombs. The act of
memory is an act of ghostwriting, a fire
in the porch of a ruined monastery.

Roadside Memorials

It's winter and in Santa Fe, people in trucks
pull over to decorate roadside memorials—

Christmas lights and plastic wreaths,
sacred candles and figurines. It seems

too festive for death, but I can understand
the impulse to visit the place of passing,

the spot where loved ones took their last
sideways glance at speeding SUVs, where

their ghosts peeled away from their bodies.
There are too many of these vigils and I'm

daily reminded of my student, just eighteen,
randomly shot in the head while driving.

I wonder if his street-side memorial
has Christmas lights. I wonder if his ghost

hovers above those nearby snowy mountains
watching cars go by like insect exoskeletons,

at night, a string of lights that just for him,
light up like fireflies.

Run Hide Fight

active shooter drill at the community college

    culinary students smothered in fake blood line the hallways
to your office

    an actor runs by yelling   firing blank shots

overhear two students talking about hunting   making elk jerky

    note their access to guns   note your own childhood access
to guns

    two weeks later   both are shot

    R. survives / Cameron dies   Cameron was your best student

see again the dead deer in your childhood backyard

    eyes wet   cut-out tongue longer than you thought it would be

    dad's hand inside her sliced-open abdomen

the unhidden gun in the back waistband of a Crown Heights neighbor

    the front of your building shot up during a quick bodega run

your old neighbors in Philly   murder / suicide

    bodies on the other side of your apartment wall

    the one your baby's crib was up against

note the lack of windows in your current classroom   the nearest exits

    the lack of makeshift weapons   just chairs and pencils

    note a student's anger at a bad grade   another student's
    grim silence

watch the Run Hide Fight video at work   remember when
Homeland Security

    was a non-existent department of government   remember when

    your job didn't require students to play dead

the deer opens her mouth wide   is trying to tell you something

    see the stump where her tongue once was

    wonder if a human shot in the head   looks that alive just
    after death

IV

The Cardinal's Language

I reached deep in you and pulled out a cardinal /
Which in bright red / Flew out the window.
   —from Dorothea Lasky's "Love Poem"

From the root of my throat,
a three-headed snapdragon,
the same feather-vermillion.

Your bird perches there,
stem bending under
its cloud weight.

It tweets its bird-speak
to the group of mute flowers,
their dragon faces

snapped shut and grimacing,
no fingers pinching their cheeks
to peek at pollen-streaked tongues.

But this is not a bestiary—
there is no medieval
symbolism or morality.

Like the plant, I do not
understand one trill
of the cardinal's language.

Without translation,
I can only watch its downy chest
puff back and forth in earnest.

Animals

Spring is roadkill season, crows
gathering in the street for lunch,
the shadow of a coyote hunched
against pueblo wall, legs limping
down the slight slope of an arroyo.

I often forget about animals until
I'm confronted by their bodies—
in Brooklyn, a dead kitten guarded
by her clan till I called sanitation,
neighbors looking the other direction,

on a Saturday morning in winter,
the lone Staten Island possum
loping across a snowy field like
an Arctic Armadillo or a giant rat,
plausible in the forgotten borough,

the trotting fox in Fort Collins,
the kind that I imagine curtsies,
wears pillbox caps with hatpins,
fans a cape of auburn fur behind her,
storybook eyes slick with awareness,

all of the bears, non-storybook,
that I have survived in campsites
and on hikes, no porridge, no chairs
or beds, just my ill-fitting bravery,
too big for my small and eatable body.

I often forget that I am one too,
a not-so-wild animal on the move.
I growl, prowl grocery store aisles,
rub my hands across my hairy legs
and mate on early morning Sundays.

Deflowering

And I leave you as a souvenir the dark, fanged rose I
plucked from between my thighs.
    —Angela Carter, "The Lady of the House of Leaves"

Lover, how many times did we try
to lose my virginity?

How many partial entries
and improvised endings?

How many joints smoked on the back-
yard couch, honeysuckle flowers

like tiny yellow trumpets, or sneaked
sips of roommate wine, all the while

the wild grapevines drooping
from the front-yard lattice?

How many hares and tortoises merely
loping through the hole in the fence?

In my small room, the daybed's tie-dye
sheets ballooning with exasperation,

we finally went through with it,
the afternoon dwindling into dusk,

a bird of paradise's shadow a black
mohawk against the window blinds—

novelty fled, yet *the flower*
did not seem to be quite dead.

The Unguessable Country of Marriage

A cento from "The Bloody Chamber"

Do not hang the bloody sheets, the sign
of a virginity so recently ruptured,
a red ribbon like the memory of a wound.

The sea has changed key—it must be
near morning. Gift of crystallized fruit,
of couloured stones, pelts of dead beasts,

undertakers' lilies with the heavy
pollen that powders your fingers as if
you had dipped them in turmeric.

How the thick glass distorted their fat
stems, possessed of that strange
ominous calm of a pond iced thickly over.

I smelled the amniotic salinity of the sea
that, in time, will cleanse everything.

A Warning

Lover, I wake you and in your stupor of sleep, you wonder aloud
why I have not yet transformed into a different creature.
What kind of monster did you dream me into being?

If I must, I will morph into a harpy like the statue in Glasgow's
Kelvingrove Museum or those pixelated half birds of a youth
spent playing *Kid Icarus* on the original NES.

I'll finally be one of those badass bitches of mythology.
You can try to attack me while I sleep, quiet and sidestepping
rows of feathers that enclose my velvet body, but if you fail,

I will breastfeed you among the blooming corpse flowers,
petals like veiny cabbage leaves that peel away from a field
of phalluses, death-musk suspended at the soil's surface.

Oh, the Places I've Pumped Breast Milk

Mostly bathrooms. Twice a week in
Staten Island Ferry restrooms peeking
at spent streetwalkers through the space
around the doorway, watching them
take off their heels and rub their soles.

I tried to minimize the sounds of suction
and the hot liquid splatter of blue milk
while choppy water bumped my shoulders
against the cold metal walls of the stall,
hurrying to finish before docking
lest I have to wear my breasts lopsided,
one soft and one hard, on the train home.

In offices and on airplanes and buses.
Once, I pumped in Edinburgh Castle's
bathroom, underground caverns
where queens and kings traversed while
chained prisoners waned in dungeons
and princesses married in the chapel—

a tiny single room where stained glass spills
multicolored light in geometric patterns.
No such thing as breast pumps then,
but working wet nurses, rough nipples
dipped into the mouths of strange babes.

I Sing the Body Elastic

Stretching back and forth like
dough in slow motion—here,
a C-section smile made Cyclops
by the flattened bellybutton—
there, ripples in the skin like
sand ruffling in a desert wind.

My body is winding around time,
a moving staircase that carries me,
full of brain and heart
through liminal terrains.

The mole on my chin
a mark asymmetric,
the fold of an ear's helix
a closed envelope un-
read and undelivered.

I am like a great Picasso painting,
squared and cubed, or a Duchamp,
nude and descending that same
staircase moving me, unwilling,
though time, through space, unpaused.

I want to slip on my high school
dance body, lithe muscles like springs,
wear my college skin, newly risqué
and high, hallucinating the body
I will wear when I'm sixty,
the loosening of all that created
other humans, gave them milk.

These are all my female forms—
kinetic, even my atoms when I am gone
will continue to reverberate, lock on
to other matter, still creating.

A Question of Wholeness

A cento from *Ghostwritten*

Paths forked off and forked off
some more. I followed the monk
through a maze of cloisters.
We came to a quiet place, a grave.
The milky turquoise vow of silence
hung white in the twilight.
I passed through a great doorway
and stood in a network of tunnels.
The music of dulcimers lit the path.
Holy Mountain, I feel like I've
climbed out of a dark box and into
quasars. There are so many cities
in every single city, sometimes
language can't even read
the music of meaning, the me
that lives in me. I'm this person,
I'm that person, I'm that person too—
tiny life-form of star compost
full of the sun and the moon.

Waiting to Be Discovered

On fog-topped mountains, streams
trickle and glimmer like zippers.
It's as if a giant could unzip them,
peel back the folds of loam to expose
long-lost artifacts—a Viking vessel
and its contents of golden brooches,
leaded and stained glass, metals
that wait centuries for detectorists.
Hidden temples wait too, their dead
saints ossified, un-canonized, eyes
replaced with sapphires, remains
laced with gold and gemstones.
The Scots imprisoned their cadavers,
graves bird-caged in wrought iron,
keeping thieves at bay. Can you
imagine all of the precious cameos,
those tiny eyes looking up at closed
caskets for eternity? Jewelry inset
with pink rubies? What other
treasures lie with the dead, wanting
to be lifted into the afterlife too?
And all of the lost torcs and lockets
and war loot just waiting to be
discovered, layer-caked, roots and
rain and earthworms the only things
grazing against them for decades.

I am in a Crater that's No More

A cento from *Kafka on the Shore*

The path from the entrance on
is spread to the horizon in a thick,
anonymous cloak of a labyrinth.

It was the ancient Mesopotamians,
they pulled out human intestines,
used the shape to predict the future.

Step into that other world. Your heart
is a mechanism buried inside of me—
the pendulum—simple, centripetal.

The moon moves the unmoving Sphinx,
becomes a knife that pierces your dreams.
Bathed by bone white light, you keep on moving.

V

Your Gun

Mike, your gun is an inscription—
it can be read right to left
like a Hebrew text. I imagine it feels
cold in the mouth and tastes
metallic. When you squatted
at my house on Rita Lane,
your gun was unreadable.
I only say this because it was
early and no amount of squinting
could help me see the blurred
language of it as it sat on my
bathroom counter, forgotten
in your inebriated state. You love
teeth-cracking drugs because
milk teeth cut gums, and mumble
things like *whore, a whore,
eternal virgins.* The wild eyes
of desperation emit a kind of dog-
like adoration from your face.
When you're high, you fly over
adobe and pueblo, saguaro and
ocotillo, over me and Tracy
picking our prickly pear's fruit
without gloves. Soon enough, you
will have a permanent landing,
abet your brother Neil when he
hides in an apartment. Later,

on the nightly news, I see a
police robot break down your door,
pursue both of you. I know that
quiet gun is on your person, that
your brother really did push
some guy in front of a train—
to him, it looked like a spaceship
hurtling toward the playground.
I overheard him say he liked it.
Your gun speaks a different tongue,
flicks each word and phrase like
a corn snake licking the wind.

Out of Town

When I'm out of town, I smoke a bowl with a stranger from the bar,

    miss my train stop and accept a ride from a man I don't know,
    figure it's statistically safer than a man I do know,

    later snub two other men's offers for rides,

    get yelled at by a drunk guy because I won't have sex with him.

They all ask, *Where are you staying?*

    I answer them vaguely.

Though I worry about my safety, I want to live like a man,

    drink at a bar without fulfilling strangers' expectations,

    walk alone wearing headphones after the bar closes,

    release the key I clutch between my fingers,
    warm in my pocket and ready to stab if necessary.

The Enemy

A cento from *Even Cowgirls Get the Blues*

The enemy is the tyranny of the dull mind
and a typewriter of birds banging out
sonnets in the dogwood buds. No,
not those crows that just haiku-ed by,
but the eyes closed tight inside
the pale blue beehive of Dakota sky,
waves of grasses whispering, and there
was the lake, laking. This sentence
is made of yak wool/sunlight and plums/ice,
and all a book contains is sentences.
When poor Jack Kerouac heard about this,
he got drunk for a week. Many small streams
empty into these pages. I never promised you
the Potomac.

Pixie

A pixie rides a rawhide worm,
the clitellum her saddle, slick
and pink as a clitoris. They maze
their way through rogue grass
until something catches her eye—
two garden snails in the distance,
wet skin catching the last flicker
of Montana sky. The pixie dismounts,
throws an arm around her earthworm
and pulls them both close to the loam.
The snails are about to couple, a rare
sight considering their hermaphroditic
nature. They move closer to each other,
lift their faces and press the bulk
of their bodies together, their sides
twisting like ribbon candy. That night,
the pixie dreams a field of snakes to life,
lies still with delight as they writhe.

Clam Honey

A cento from *Even Cowgirls Get the Blues*

Sissy, your thumb disorients us—
you hitchhike bees, snakes,
clouds, dandelion puffs of
the cosmic pumpkin.
What looks to be a wisp of cloud
is actually the moon, narrow
and pale like a navel, wrinkled
and cupped, whorled
and domed. I am the jewel
in its lotus. Rise above
phosphorescence, O vagina!
Your salty incense, your
mushroom moon musk,
your deep waves of clam honey
breaking against the cold
steel of civilization
that was willing to put
a matter as delicate as this
in the kitten-crusher hands
of the police. About the time
the steam calliope was wheezing,
a mean mad icesnake of a wind
could make you smell
the rising tide of toadstool.

Cowgirls

The arrow in my tongue is a Doric column
that butts against my palette the way a
buttress props a cornice, and all of this is to say
that I am thinking about the way a pat of butter
surrenders down the side of hot corn on the cob.
Butter, room temperature, is like eating the sun,
slips the way cold does up the bottom of Sissy
Hankshaw's coat on Manhattan mornings.
But Sissy's at the ranch and elsewhere, lumberjacks
play Swedish fiddles for twerking acorns.
Someone is shaving a stag's antlers for smelling salts.
The ashy hartshorn of the universe drips pitch
like a parched riverbed below the ghosts of cowgirls.
Bonanza Jellybean tips her hat and knows that
I'll never visit that ditch again. The candy mines
shut down—the U.S. Mint lacked flavor. But that
doesn't mean that I can't hunt like a great archer,
bowstring between fingers pulled to meet my cheek.

American Cliff Swallows

American Cliff Swallows
have taken over my portico,
their lumpy mud nests
popping up in every corner.
When I open my front door,
they whisk out of small holes
and circle my head, wings
curved and pointed like a
ship's bow, pastel yellow
bellies swooping just feet
above me. As a house renter,
I wonder if I'm expected to
knock down these mud caves,
evict these tenets with broom
in hand like a crazy landlady.
I'm afraid to ask, so I don't.
My children's babysitter acts
like we are the chosen ones,
specially anointed as if
I have been presented with
a rug of artifacts and have
correctly chosen the bell, but
sometimes, it feels more like
being in a cult. I can't escape
their tweets and squeaks
and worry they'll take over
the house if they get inside.

All I can do is close the door
quickly behind me and hope
that they migrate before the
homeowner returns.

The Parade

*Where the plaza is, where Santa Fe is, pueblos once
stood. They walk on our blood and bones every day.*
                    —Pueblo activist Jennifer Marley

New to Santa Fe, my family and I participate
in a children's parade during Fiestas, a time
to celebrate the Spanish. We throw candy
to bystanders and smile and wave. It isn't until
we approach the end when I begin to realize,
seeing Spanish descendants dressed like royalty,
that this parade glorifies Diego de Vargas'
so-called "bloodless reconquest." Only then
do I comprehend that I am celebrating
the murder of Pueblo people—seventy men
killed, women and children enslaved.
But families in bright ruffled clothing cheer
at the Palace of the Governors, where the ears,
and later, bodies, of resisters were hanged.
We are not just walking, but dancing even
over the blood and bones of the Pueblo.
I shrink with my hot white-idiot shame
as protesters are arrested and dragged away
from the very place their ancestors were slaves.

Old Man Gloom

Every year, Santa Feans burn Zozobra, an effigy stuffed with people's gloom.

Dear Old Man Gloom,
this country has abandoned
my cunt, the Paris Agreement,
seventy-two provisions for
people's special needs' babies
and I'm still stung about
Brandon Teena and Matthew
and everyone else whose face
flashes across the news like
a yearbook of the dead. I try
not to think about he-who-
must-not-be-named, but
his hate keeps rolling through
my head—too much *blood
coming out of her eyes* and
grab them by the pussy. More
politicians are outed as predators
but not ousted. Men shoot
babies in churches and gun
stocks grow more valuable.
Police shoot Black people and
get paid leave. Zozobra, some
of my gloom will burn within you,
some of it will stay within me.

I will witness the last puff
of smoke rising from your papier-
mâché body, prepare myself
for another year's injustice.

History

A cento from *Even Cowgirls Get the Blues*

The first amoebae that ever lived
is still alive. It weeps for the decline

of poets, tumbleweed, the peyote
wagon, the distant buttes and canyons,

the sky full of blades grinning
like piranha in their cases.

The mastodons are all gone; so are
the Amazons. Timbuktu is now

a roadside zoo so grand and giant
and elegant that your heart

squeezed out eternity's toothpaste
so early the bluebirds hadn't brushed their teeth yet.

History isn't ever going to end.
And history is ending every second.

When We Look at the Night Sky

We see the past, the celestial
bodies of family members
that have already died.

Everything swirls & darkles in spirals.
Pull each skin layer back, glimpse
epochs and lake pores

pocked along granite and all
of our past selves forking
into paths of crab grass,

even the ghosts of our future children
frolicking on tick-infested trails,
shrubbery-lined, thistled,

and/or looking over tiny shoulders
calling from the schoolyard for us,
always for us to come back,

drag them by the hand into the present.

Notes

(where they apply in chronological order)

I

"From Our Apartment Window, My Son Sees a Planet": The phrase "an unlearn'd astronomer" is a play on Walt Whitman's poem title "When I Heard the Learn'd Astronomer."

"A Dream": The epigraph comes from an art piece displayed in Glasgow's Botanic Gardens called "Bromeliad (Commissioned Memorial)" by Ruth Barker.

"Thunderbird Egg": All lines from this poem are taken from Louise Erdrich's 2012 novel *The Roundhouse*.

II

"High Desert": The epigraph comes from Larry Levis' poem "Ghazal" from his book *The Darkening Trapeze: Last Poems* published posthumously in 2016.

"Silence, I Discover, is Something You Can Actually *Hear*": All lines from this poem are taken from Haruki Murakami's 1999 novel *Kafka on the Shore*.

"Comings and Goings": All lines from this poem are taken from Louise Erdrich's 2012 novel *The Roundhouse*.

"Until I Come Back": All lines from this poem are taken from the films *Secretary*, *Bad Education*, *Videodrome*, *The Pillow Book*,

Rudderless, The Science of Sleep, Palindromes, Being John Malkovich, Fear and Loathing in Las Vegas, Drop Dead Fred, The Big Lebowski, Donnie Darko, and *The Young and Prodigious T.S. Spivet.*

"Poem in Which I Address Two Chatbots": The transcripts of robot dialogue this poem references can be found on *The Telegraph's* website.

III

"Drunk on Opals": This title is taken from a line in David Mitchell's 2002 novel *Ghostwritten.*

"It's Lonely to Be Alive and Never Know the Whole Story": All lines from this poem are taken from Eileen Myles' 1994 novel *Chelsea Girls.*

"Color": This poem, after Philip Larkin's poem "Water," came from an exercise given by Tony Hoagland during his final seminar series in Santa Fe, 2017.

"Your Chair": Cameron Martinez was my student at the University of New Mexico's Los Alamos campus when he was killed.

"A Crow or a Poet": All lines from this poem are taken from David Mitchell's 2002 novel *Ghostwritten.*

"Run Hide Fight": This title refers to the video *RUN. HIDE. FIGHT.® Surviving an Active Shooter Event* put out by the FBI.

IV

"The Cardinal's Language": The epigraph comes from Dorothea Lasky's "Love Poem" from her book *Awe* published in 2007.

"Deflowering": The title and the closing italicized words are from Angela Carter's story "The Lady of the House of Love" included in her 1979 short story collection *The Bloody Chamber*.

"The Unguessable Country of Marriage": All lines from this poem are taken from Angela Carter's short story "The Bloody Chamber" included in her 1979 short story collection *The Bloody Chamber*.

"A Question of Wholeness": All lines from this poem are taken from David Mitchell's 2002 novel *Ghostwritten*.

"I am in a Crater that's No More": All lines from this poem are taken from Haruki Murakami's 1999 novel *Kafka on the Shore*.

V

"Your Gun": This poem came from an exercise called 20 Little Poetry Projects by Jim Simmerman published in *The Practice of Poetry*, edited by Robin Behn and Chase Twitchell in 1992.

"The Enemy": All lines from this poem are taken from Tom Robbins' 1976 novel *Even Cowgirls Get the Blues*.

"Clam Honey": All lines from this poem are taken from Tom Robbins' 1976 novel *Even Cowgirls Get the Blues*.

"The Parade": This poem references the children's parade called

Desfile de los Niños during the week of Fiestas de Santa Fe.

"Old Man Gloom": This poem references the burning of Zozobra, an almost century-long artist-created event where Santa Feans stuff a huge effigy called Zozobra with their "gloom" and then burn it during the week of Fiestas de Santa Fe.

"History": All lines from this poem are taken from Tom Robbins' 1976 novel *Even Cowgirls Get the Blues*.

About the Author

In addition to *A New Kind of Tongue*, Genevieve Betts is also the author of the poetry collection *An Unwalled City* (Prolific Press, 2015). Her work has appeared in *Sleet Magazine*, *Minerva Rising*, *Cloudbank*, *Sky Island Journal*, *New Mexico Review*, *Hotel Amerika*, *The Literary Review*, and in other journals and anthologies. She is an assistant professor of English at Santa Fe Community College and teaches creative writing for Arcadia University's low-residency MFA program. She lives in Santa Fe, New Mexico.

CPSIA information can be obtained
at www.ICGtesting.com
Printed in the USA
JSHW032238200723
45010JS00006B/20